MW01226778

FOR CREATIVE NONFICTION: This is a work of creative nonfiction. Some parts have been fictionalized in varying degrees, for various purposes

ISBN: 979-8-9858513-0-4

Written By: Shanah Holland (Heavens Gold), Nevaeh Holland, Patricia Holland,

Cover Art and Interior Editing: Gates Creative Group

Cover Photography: Alan Daher

THE EP

This EP is dedicated to my one and Only sibling Charles Holland Jr. We all we got!

My Heaven Bound Daddy, Charles Holland.
My Earth Bound Queen, Patricia Holland.
With all the love, reverence and gratitude.

I am grateful for my children's undying support and love for me. I will always be here even when I'm not.
My spiritual and soul healer Willie Hayes Jr. Your love has shifted my growth. I'm forever grateful.

To My incredible, incomparable team Sheena Gates & Brad Baker.
if it were not for you two this book may not have seen the light of someone's way.

A special acknowledgement to my Nephew, Azeem & Niece, Ashanti.
Titi said you can do anything you put your mind to.

Do you Believe me now?

- Titi

I was asked to write this not knowing how or what to actually say. But I know the author so this will be easy... or so I thought.. At least it should be.

Complex, defiant, always reliant and ever evolving.

Heaven's Gold speaks from the heart. Hurt, Pain, Love, Loss, Death, Birth, Rebirth. It's all told through words that will soothe your soul. Wherever you've been or wherever you're going this heartfelt compilation will allow you to reflect on your own personal experiences. Only through the journey do we understand that our lives are not our own. Our trials are for the building of our faith. Faith in our creator who sets each one of us on a path to fulfill what has been predestined and in turn to share with the world. That is the beginning of healing.

That is where we find Heaven, and it is Gold.

Love, Momma ♥

Patricia Holland

The EP

God's Math
Sugar High
Self Doubt (ed)
Cool Crush
Peace
Back in the Day
Yin & Yang
Pressure
Homage (Flowers)
Kept Frozen
Ransom: Pay with your Life
New Wreckless Order
Dream Chasers
Scared Love
Goddess Created
Akkkirema (Amerikkka)
Longitude & Latitude
Dear Parental
Kneel: The pa$n ain't cheap
I'm not a rapper
My Purpose
Transparent Type

Gods Math

Speak what you want
God is ready to deliver.
That is the God in you that you choose to invest and
make the winner.
See we are all a part of the math.

The equation? Simple.
You minus ego plus God,

Seek guidance & proper salvation.
The only gps on cue.

God has my eyes & you know who got the wheel.
I ain't driving
Just know Goddess ascendant is all I rise in.

No surprises
No frills
Or sugar to coat ya feels

Just real recognizing the very real
aspects of how to heal.

Small circles
Less talk
More build.

No destroying the throne

God blesses the child with the ability to curate they
own.

Sugar High

Watch for the sugar high of emotions that's ready to crash like oceans.

Watch for the desperate version of who you wanna be.

Stay potent.

Love on yourself entirely.
Melt your own heart into GOLD heavily.

Shine bright like the star you are.

Where excellence meets YOUR truest goddess essence.

No fear. All signs so clear.

Peace always flows better from within.

Draw them near.

Self Doubt

Self-doubt almost killed me.

My momma's words in talks of aborting me.

Self doubted the strength of me.

Self loathed the thought that she would fail in a pattern like her momma before me.

She showed up when I arrived in the same form as her mother, treacherously.

Silence in fear, unable to speak.

Words play like memory reels on my mind's projectory.

How she hurt and can't see the hurt in me.

How she sage but caged the ideas in me.

How she so new now but can't get to her truest self.

Revealing her wounds gave birth to my legacy.

For you are me.

(Nevaeh's Voice)

Cool Crush

My floor is someone's ceiling.

He said in our daily verbiage in
Circa 1800's poetry like literally.

He don't even try to be.
He gravitates to my cool
But he's my crush you see eye sparkles so bright I see
all three .

I wanna fly just above his plight and save his world you
see.

I'm not any woman's threat
and not just any man's fantasy.

Between my eyes resides
in high vibrant delicacy.

A mind to outshine the seas.

I for you and you for me.

We
Need
Not
A
Thing.

Peace

. The pride in your stride,
the way you graciously commanded our hand
unknowingly centering us.
aligning our chakras
You are peace.
You are Shiloh.
You are a part of our lineage
Guard us in the Godly dimensions above
Keep our peace on earth together as pure as your
presence.
We've gleaned.
We aren't apart from you
Your soul dispersed into us all.
Our eternal love will forever bond us together.

Love your sister human.

Back in The Day

When Barbie was the wave
Cousins was ya only circle
Hair beads adorned your crown
And no worries for the warriors was allowed.

Back in the days when numbers were exaggerated and
dress up was a hairbrush,
comb, and maybe two outfit switch up for ya doll baby.

Back in the days when loving yourself wasn't a risk

Your smile was a gift.

Laughter was a true medicinal lift.

In those days I was so sure of my being.

Complete in my position
Now sometimes strangely I'm speaking and unsure of
my reasons.

My uplift is watching the youth on their missions
in they own world control of their feelings.

That's a real dreamers beginning.

Ying & Yang

Keep the sorrow in rotation by curving actions of meditation

Curbing acting's of meditation keeps the sorrow in rotation
Negative ascended, all I ask is you listen.

You Balance out my yang & yin even ask permission it's over for ya provisions I get it.

Positive.

I'm positively gifted in writing our ass out this vision of life.

This book needs no denunciations.
I'll twist the script still staying in fruition

My lane however it split will be HOV lane provisions.

I'm on a mission.

Pressure

So there's this man that I Stan I mean imma a fan.

This man is deeply complex and caramel in skin.

This man who's full of man, beauty surpasses a 10.

This man, this hue of a man in colors he's a conundrum.

In my eyes, he's a gift.

So to this man that I Stan I mean imma a fan.

Be bright. Be light. Be better than.

Be transparent in honoring.
Be present in thought.
Be intentional in speech.

Be able to reach new heights.
This work of a man is right.

Godlike.

Heaven sent.

To my full extent, I will pray over your steps.
To this man that I stan I mean imma fan

I've waited all night.
Let's take this flight.
I feel we might be true.
We could be new.
Few lovers lovin like you.

If it's not you then who?
If it's you then we should be
Manifesting a rich-filled destiny.
A whole-souled pleasantry
Love in wide lenses.

Voices melodically invested.
Intentionally vetted. Respected.

Built a Home in your very essence.

Rooms way too expressant.

I think I'm in like , y'all.

Homage Flowers

It's Black Men that's educated and
Queens like Gabriella
singing we made it.

I know it's my time.

Black shinned & I'll do the dishes.

Great dinner.
Cleaned the pots and pans.

While I hum tunes from Muva Badu or Queen Jill
Mixed wit Sha-Roc in her freedom trance I'll write my 16
version of a poets penial gland.

My position is a healer's hand I'm realer than what you
can think.

So as you can.
Be at peace but a beast within.

I'm no rapper I just flow calmer than a Rivers bend

Highly I ascend

You love my presence and it shows within.

I'm golden and my home is heaven.

Kept Frozen

I thought this feeling was just an interlude.

Telescope views I would alter my universe for you.

Intentions to paper
Origami folds
Burned in the sky to you.

This show, mine only.
Captions only

Forgive me how I've managed to cultivate everything I
ever wanted in the imagery of fantasy.

This hold is real.
I can't fake it.
Shake it.
Or deal.

Maybe I just need to heal.

Way too comfortable with you but who knew?

Colors would exude.
What a beautiful and rare hue.

Man, you took all my cool.
A little of my sanity too.
My imagination got me through seasons with you.
Can you miss someone you never met or even knew?

I'll forever keep our connection graceful.

Keep you clean.

No bowls broken.

No gold fills to cracks.

BLACK MEN DON'T CHEAT

I gotcha back.

Ransom
Pay with your life

20 years old with two in dresses.

Life is what you make it Queen get lit to the lessons.

They say what they want
but it's ours they hate our greatness.

Get paid off the top
men and women lie
so let's keep the arrangement
the power of now in modulation.

Your soul and how you ascend in is your validation.

My God takes better care of me, I need no part of ya
currency made to hate and twerk on key my mind
is changing the weather I give instruction to
my seeds through ritual love letters.

I am divinely curated.

My lane I'm creating it paving it
don't dare tell me to stay
in it.

I'll be in yours too

Fly over the whole crew.
Give verbal lashings out to mumble
niggas let's call it they just due.

Dream Chaser

Last night the same dream had me gifting my niece her first Grammy.

When I woke I changed the narrative.

Soul settings I told God I got the message.

No karmic debt. Not wreckless.

No evil intent.

No masking this.

Heavy on the real.

I got this I foot the bill.

Life moving it's my time.

Nothing gon stop this

Heavy on what's mine.

Goddess Created

All ya greats have a funny tooth smile.

Nigga I'm cute.
Cole, Nas
even the Goat'll
tell you.

"They'll laugh at you then
cry for you."

What that hate-driven admiration'll prove.
Block me cause of ya
visual, personal point
of view.

Only blockin the message
that's hella reckless.

Words truer
from the great Ms. Hill
Spoken With heavy aggression.

"The world ya made is what ya left with"

You see I'm Picture perfect
Just not how Yoncè finesse it.
This verbal dope that I flood ya eardrums with is hope.

So you have more to use to cope
more to intake speak life through ya throat.

My writing creates to expose
only the bare necessities of my soul.

I'm transparent.

Like Em & Mekhi
Told on miles of
build & destroy
that raised an ego.

I'm golden
Like Jill be living her life.

I'm never folding
Like Hov spoke at the end of a gangsta tale.

So sweet like my momma banana puddin'.

This is my heaven

I'm unique
I'm rather me.

Akkkirema (Amerikkka)

Freedom papers turned to birth certificates yet still, we holler
for the importance of black lives on US soil.

Yea we built this here we not leaving.
We also not feeding ourselves on our own.

Can't produce crops but pop hips and pack bundles of horse
tresses to block our crowns from ancestral blessings,
whispers and confessings we don't get those.

Just vultures who wanna profit off how our fit goes.

How we commit loads of magical scenarios from the hell of project ghettos.

How goes that experiment anyway?

Too many now a billi richer from experience
Ya don't say.

Time to inject our babies with the what's to say
and blame it on the slanty eyes we made to pay.

My correction will never be polite or political.

So Phuk ya emotions or comments on tonight.

I bathe in the ingredients, I'm edible arranged.

My mind deliciously served with ice.

I am the change.

Longitude & Latitude

Deeper looks like drowning to the hurt and down.
My breathing apparatuses accoutred while I sit
OHM style on the ocean ground.

Falling in love in you like falling in the wild.
Up the Highest mountain cliffs.

Peninsula drip
I'm your fountain.

Not left in ignorance or ever dismissed
his love is deeper.

Deeper I'm going
Deep
Deep
Deep in this.

Under ocean floors and beyond the heat coils
Earths pearly gated door.

Humans don't know this depth it's too real, takes too long.

They Latitude foreign.

My whole soul grabbed your pieces
and restored you to your thrown.

My deeper love reacher made us reborn.

Dear Parentats

Dear, (hue)man's

To admire the painting and not the painter Stifles me.

You say you love Me and you don't believe in God
Well, that doesn't look like love to me.

The more of you that you love
is God you see
Even God needs us.
To realize the
Beauty of we.

All the paintings have been created for all to see.

Born Daily like a ritual crying to love he.

Or she for that matter.

The nurturing ritual is that of a mother's delightful platter.

Cleanings and seasonings to name a few.

How God really does care for the beautiful things we view.

My eyes are a blessing I won't regret or take for granted

What I have access to

I am loved and listened to

Kneel
The Pa$n aint cheap

Don't eliminate your chances to be the best you
stand on ya own two.

You only got one leg well stand proud with the gift
that God still kept you.

Don't fear God's breath is in you.

Don't ever sell yourself cheap, my pain looped for two decades.

My books are 444 degrees over cypher.

Pain now defeated.

Orient ya presence with the habit of ya favorite hustler
success is what you produce package and deliver.

Freedom over culture.

It's more in me though.

That's why you seeing, hearing ,and feel deep in ya soul.

My timing is right.

Bare witness and get hit with this Queens glow.

I'm not a rapper

I'm not a rapper I'm a writer
Wrote out my soul's recovery.
Fluently speak Nas, Hov & Big's parlance
Graduated poetically.

I'm a writer.
I am a poet.

A muhphukin prophet among us.
With one book out of a million publishings.

Bet it be classically viewed like reasonable doubt.
Since y'all doubted me.

Through the cadence of our greatest
My life is Connected to greatness!

To prove it, I manifest THEY hands to help move it.
ONLY BUILT FOR GOD'S TO ATTUNE TO IT!

A divinely placed GODDESS will do it!

We are not the same. I want NOT the fame.

Only to famously BREAK THE BANK.

I'm this intentional or rather I'm that hood.

Plus I know my Ingenious pen leave well-versed rappers
egregiously stank.

So that hate that's in ya kids & ya mate.

We can't relate.
It's hard to stomach the simulated peasantry of self-doubt

Flowin from out ya face
We ova here being greats!

My Purpose

Great minds discuss brilliant ideas
Preparation meeting determination with no fear.

It is in you
like it's in me
like it's in the billionaire's heir.
Eye can change the polarity of 90 thousand Hurt souls
Hawkins law prevails
What is your purpose in life?
What is a life of nothing but chasing the bag blind?
In God who trusts?
That wording I don't abide
As for self,
In trust for God eye
uplift the frequency
so my Funds are a tool
wasn't in my momma to raise fools.
We've queen'd & king'd from systemic hoods, schooling & thinking. Stop
looping hurt, twerking, and being blue
Just vibrate ya hue.
die empty from prolifically pouring ya purpose to the youth. The all-seeing
eye is you.
What is your purpose in life?

All I need...

I am the chick that hold the bliky

Like don't Phuk wit me

My kids or my pennies

Now understands we can't be stopped

From overseas to Richmond

And back to Jersey

Like we undergrowth and dirty

Not me.

A nigga been focused since I said bye to my daddy

Inner Youngin will never be hurt again

Better watch an learn something.

"And learn how to earn better"

I burn the set up.

I set fire to your simulation of desires

I blow smoke in your face, burn rubber off of rim tires."

Yes I am a Goddess living. DOUBLE BLESSED UP

Taking all my stolen goods back.

Holland Back!

Transparent Type

I had the iMac desktop in graphite.
Queen been the transparent type

In hindsight I shoulda shared
more of my light.

But I feel like all y'all would do is hate & bite.

Find ways to make me shame my display.

It's funny how y'all speak damnation on life
But can't do the same thing.
Win the game
Jump like J
Score like Kobe
Or make a stadium scream ya name

Do you baby
you ain't in my way.

My lane paved, caved
Not one for the needs of y'all live sessions.

But don't test her.

She's in her prime
There's no telling
What she didn't get to address'n

Or where that'll even go
Who knows
With the brilliance she shows,
she can shift the globe .

Make a Black millionaire row
or converse with the minister.

To change our souls I ascended with this energy
Way before you knew what you know.

I'm Gil Scotts soul
born on Bernie mac's birthday.

I'm truth spewed
dipped in gold.

Look at me.

I'm ya favorite writers retina
Ya hottest rappers healer.

I apologize for not knowing I was me.
It altered a lot of y'all feelings
Time for healing.

God getting with me
But for now, I'll chastise the Queens
Tweakin if you twerkin and you broke.

Nah Nas I can't leave em alone.
Too much greatness in us as a whole.

Individually holy
We are the ancestry.

Goddesses and Gods we are so, of course,
they want it to look like we
hate the very ground that made us we.
We know better than that

We had the miseducation of Ms. Hill
It wasn't placed vainly.

From The Artist

What is your purpose in life?
I wake up with this question in my mouth after a praise(of course.)
EVERY MORNING.
With this EP its imbedded. I've made it made up my mind I
want epochal stories to this legendary legacy I'm living, Eye Invision
helping others not just working around others.
I vow to create concrete CHANGE in MYSELF not just my environment or
financials.
I desire authentic connection not just spectators & energy vampires

I am intentional.
Hella intentionally.
These poems serve as tools
My purpose is to cultivate my Heaven. You coming with?

From The Artist

Thank you for listening to your soul I hope you enjoy this occasion ☆

In the famous words of Frankie Beverly.
"There's a time in your life when you find WHO YOU ARE
That's the Golden time of day"

Heavens
GOLD